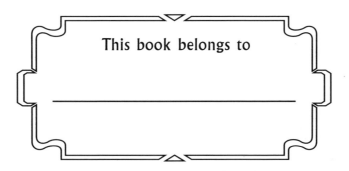

This book belongs to

_____

CHARACTERS

Buffalo Biff - Asa Wiggins
Ruby - Katie Stewart
Pete - Mathew Walters
Theodore Roosevelt - Robert White Johnson

Recorded by: Open Door Productions
Talent Directed by: Brian T. Cox/Don Jarvis
Executive Producer: Cheryl J. Hutchinson
Developed and Created by: Toy Box Productions
Story Written by: James Collins
Art Direction and Character Illustrations by:
Brian T. Cox, for Toy Box Productions

Manufactured exclusively by
CRT, Custom Products, Inc.
Ⓟ © 2006 Toy Box Productions,
A Division of CRT, Custom Products, Inc.
7532 Hickory Hills Court
Whites Creek, TN 37189

1-800-750-1511   www.crttoybox.com

1-932332-60-X

Welcome to another Time Traveler's adventure.

We're headed back to witness the amazing life of Theodore Roosevelt, our 26th President of the United States.
He accomplished extraordinary things in his lifetime.

Hold on as we blast off with

Buffalo Biff and Farley's Raiders!

Picking a President

Ruby: I'm too young for all this homework.

Biff: What's the matter, Ruby?

Ruby: By Monday, everyone in our class has to pick a different United States President to write a report on.

Pete: That's why I already made my choice. I don't want to waste all weekend on reading and research.

Ruby: Most of the good ones are already taken. It'll be hard to write a report on a boring President.

Biff: I know a fascinating President. Has anyone picked Theodore Roosevelt?

Ruby:	No. I'll go back in class and tell the teacher that he's my choice. But I don't know much about him. He'd better be interesting.
Pete:	I'll stop by the school library and check out a book on him for you.
Ruby:	Thanks Pete. I'll see you guys in a few minutes. Hold the bus for me.
Pete:	If he's as fascinating as you say, Biff, maybe I'll check out a book on him.
Biff:	If you and Ruby start reading about him on the bus ride home, I think you'll see what I mean. I've got a better idea. Let's go on a time traveling adventure tomorrow.
Pete:	All right. Then we can see for ourselves.

Adjusting The Time Machine

Ruby: Sorry. I stayed up late reading about Theodore Roosevelt and overslept.

Pete: I've only read the introduction of my book, but this looks like an action packed trip. We may have to speed through some events.

Biff: Ruby, finish tightening these bolts. While you and Pete finish that, tell me what you've learned so far. I want to set a course and need the right time frame.

Ruby: Well, Theodore Roosevelt was born on October 27, 1858 in New York City. He was the first United States President born in a big city.

Pete: He was born with such severe asthma that no one expected him to survive.

Ruby: He had a strong father who taught him to take care of his own health and to always help the less fortunate.

Biff: It must have worked. That sick little boy became healthy enough to become a cowboy, a soldier, and a politician who became the youngest president. He was also a naturalist and an explorer who found the time to write over thirty books.

Pete: His father died when he was at Harvard University. They were very close. Two years later, he married his college sweetheart, and worked in the New York City legislature.

Ruby: One day while working outside of New York City, he received a telegram that his wife had given birth to a baby girl. He took a train home but when he got there, both his wife and mother, who lived in the same house, were very sick. The next morning his mother died of typhoid fever and later that same day his wife died of kidney failure.

Biff: All that tragedy in one day was too much for him. So, he went west and became a cowboy in the Badlands of the Dakotas. This helped him overcome his grief.

Ruby: When he returned home two years later, he bumped into his childhood friend, Edith. They fell in love and got married in 1886.

Pete:	When Mr. Roosevelt was appointed the Police Commissioner of New York City, he wanted every policeman to be able to read and write and be trained in the safe and proper use of weapons. He started a school to make sure these new standards were accomplished.
Ruby:	The school later became the New York City Police Academy.
Biff:	Then, President McKinley appointed Roosevelt as the Assistant Secretary of the Navy.
Pete:	Everything is tight on this side. Are we ready to go?
Biff:	Yes. Based on what you've told me, we should start in 1898. That's when his life really takes off into high gear. Are you coming Farley?
Farley:	Bark! Bark!
Ruby:	Come on then.
Biff:	The course is set. We've got a lot of great history to speed through, so buckle up!
All:	Yahoo!

Cuba Harbor

Pete: Wow! That's a pretty big battleship.

Ruby: Where are we?

Biff: This is a harbor in Cuba. That's the battleship, USS Maine.

Ruby: It's so beautiful here. Peaceful and quiet.

BOOM !

Ruby: What happened to that ship?

Pete: I recall that many Americans wanted the old Spanish Empire out of North America.

Biff: That's right, Pete. Many people were blaming Spain. Within two months the United States and Spain were at war. But no one ever proved what caused the ship to blow up.

The Rough Riders

Ruby: Why did Mr. Roosevelt resign from his job? Doesn't he have a wife and children?

Pete: I think he wanted to serve his country and become a war hero.

Biff: Yes. He accepted a rank of Lieutenant Colonel and organized his own regiment of cavalry.

Pete: He called them the Rough Riders.

Pete: This must be the famous charge up San Juan Hill.

Biff: San Juan was actually the second hill the Rough Riders charged that day. It was hard fighting. They lost a lot of their men.

Ruby: Spain surrendered soon after this battle, right?

Biff: Yes. I'm surprised historians even call this a war. There were less than fifty days of actual fighting.

Biff: Now, this man is Tom Platt, the leader of the Republican Party for the State of New York.

Pete: He wants Mr. Roosevelt, the war hero, to run for Governor.

Theodore Roosevelt: I accept your offer. I will run for Governor, but only if I can appoint qualified men who can perform their jobs properly.

Biff: As Governor of New York, Theodore Roosevelt wanted new laws for factories and tenement workshops.

Pete: What's a tenement workshop?

Biff: A tenement workshop is where people lived and worked in the same room.

Ruby: I'm glad he improved working conditions for so many people.

Pete: All his work for social justice made Governor Roosevelt very popular with the people.

Ruby: That must be one of the reasons why President McKinley asked Governor Roosevelt to become his Vice President when he ran for re-election.

Biff: Yes, but an awful thing happened. Seven months later into his second term, President McKinley was assassinated.

Ruby: That's a sad way for a Vice President to become President.

The Changing Face Of America

Biff: By 1901, America had changed quite a bit.

Pete: I'll say. Most of the farms near the cities were disappearing. Industries and businesses were replacing them.

Ruby: Most of the people thought all these new industries were making too much profit, while the workers were making very little money.

Biff: Many of these companies joined together. Each group of businesses were called a Trust. President Roosevelt feared this growing imbalance between the trusts and the workers might lead to some kind of uprising or revolution.

Pete: So, he decided to take action against the powerful trusts.

HARD TIMES FOR FARMERS

Biff: Many of these trusts were owned by J.P. Morgan. He was the most powerful businessman in the country.

Pete: It seems one of the purposes of these trusts was to control prices and destroy competition.

Biff: Yes. President Roosevelt didn't want any Trust, private company or individual to be considered an equal power to the Federal Government.

Ruby: I admire people who take action on what they believe.

Pete: His actions certainly made the office of the President stronger.

Biff: Most of the Presidents before Roosevelt only issued statements, made plans or offered suggestions to Congress.

Ruby: Oh, this kind of work looks dangerous, messy and sad.

Biff: The Biffometer says this is 1902. The whole country depended on coal. If the miners go on strike, it might create a national disaster for homes and businesses.

Pete: What did the miners want?

Biff: Safer working conditions, better pay and shorter working hours.

Pete: President Roosevelt called the mine workers and mine owners together to discuss the situation.

Theodore Roosevelt: I felt sorry for the miners when the owners spoke to them like they were dogs. These owners were arrogant and wouldn't cooperate at all. So, I told the Secretary of the Army to prepare some troops to take control of the mines. In this way, the miners could still work and the country would still have its coal.

Biff: With the President firmly on the side of the miners, the owners gave in.

Ruby: I think it's amazing that there was a twelve hour work day. At least this reduced it to nine.

Teddy's Bear

Pete: What's the matter, Farley?

Biff: The President went hunting but had no luck. So, someone found a bear and tied it to a post. President Roosevelt refused to shoot the poor thing.

Ruby: Don't worry Farley. They set the bear free. Some reporter told the story and his paper printed this cartoon. Why is this important?

Biff: A toy maker saw the cartoon and stopped calling his stuffed bears toys. He started calling them Teddy's Bear. They were a big hit all across the nation. Within a year the name was changed to Teddy Bears.

Pete: That's what we still call them today.

President refuses to shoot the poor thing.

After a few unsuccessful days with no bears in sight, hunting guides finally found an old bear. The dogs ~~he~~ followed it for a long distance until the bear ~~tried~~ to escape. After the dogs attacked and ~~bit the~~ bear, the guides tied it to a tree and ~~~~ telling him they had a bear for ~~~~ President looked at the poor ~~~~ will shoot this old bear ~~~~ However, the bear ~~~~ ident ordered ~~~~ d its pain

31

Pete: The distance from New York to San Francisco, around South America, was thirteen thousand miles. The president wanted to connect the Atlantic and Pacific with a canal.

Ruby: A canal would cut the distance to only about five thousand miles.

Biff: It's hard to imagine this great engineering feat happened in the nineteen hundred's.

United States

South America

The Panama Canal

Biff: The Governor of Colombia refused a ten million dollar offer for a six mile stretch of land in their Panama province.

Pete: Why? Were they holding out for more money?

Biff: Yes. They knew a French company had tried to build a canal and failed and President Roosevelt had offered that company forty million dollars for all the equipment left behind.

Ruby: Someone told the President that rebels in Panama wanted to leave Colombia and form their own country and if they were successful, they would accept his offer

Pete: So instead of offering the Colombian government more money, he waited to see if the uprising was successful? That's pretty outrageous!

Biff: When it was successful, he recognized the new government within forty-eight hours, and paid them ten million dollars for the land needed to build the canal.

Ruby: By holding out for more money, the nation of Colombia not only lost a part of their country, they lost the money for it, too.

Theodore Roosevelt: The price was fair. I'll let Congress debate the legality and I will have the Panama Canal built.

Biff: Teddy Roosevelt was the first President to leave the United States and travel to other countries while he was in office.

Pete: The shape of the land made it extremely difficult to build.

Biff: It was quite an undertaking. Many thousands of people lost their lives while it was being built and the canal wasn't completed until after his term as President.

Ruby: But he'll always be remembered for building the Panama Canal. Let's follow him back to Washington D.C.

Fun and Laughter At The White House

Ruby: Edith, the President's wife, remodeled the White House.

Biff: Technically, it was still called the Executive Mansion. Once it was finished, the President started calling it 'The White House.'

Pete: This was the first time in many years that kids were running around. They filled the halls with laughter and pillow fights. They were famous for their water balloon fights.

Ruby: Even the President joined in! It's funny when the kids miss each other and hit the guards.

Biff: Even though some people in his own political party didn't like him, President Roosevelt was wildly popular with the people. He easily won re-election.

Pete: After his re-election, Theodore may have weakened his power to change things by telling the people that he would not seek another term after this one.

Theodore Roosevelt: I will honor the two term tradition and not run for President in the next election.

Biff: There was no official term limit. As popular as he was, he could have been President many times.

Pete: Let's see what the computer says about his second term.

Biff: I'm driving. You and Ruby look it up.

Pete: He continued to battle the Medical Trust and passed a Pure Food and Drug Act.

Ruby: He set up a Department of Commerce and Labor to protect people from unhealthy meat. He also helped farmers lower the shipping expenses of their agriculture products.

Pete: I think he transformed the Nation more by being a naturalist.

Ruby: How did he do that?

Biff: Forests were being cut down, the grasslands of the mid-west were getting ruined and the buffalo were slaughtered to near extinction. He publicly protected over two hundred thirty million acres by setting up four National Game Preserves, five new National Parks, eighteen National Monuments, fifty-one Federal Bird Reservations and one hundred fifty National Forests.

Pete: In 1907, Congress had to pass a law to allow timber to be cut, but President Roosevelt kept protecting the land.

Ruby: He was an amazing President. I have plenty of information for a school report now. What else could he have possibly done?

Biff: Well, he won the Nobel Peace Prize for ending a war between Japan and Russia.

Pete: What's all this trouble in the streets of America all about?

Biff: Oh, this is the panic of 1907. There was trouble on Wall Street. Stocks were out of control, prices collapsed, and interest rates soared. He also challenged Congress for more reforms. He wanted child labor laws, worker's compensation, an eight hour work day and social security pensions.

Ruby & Pete: WOW!

Biff: Most of these changes didn't happen right away and were passed by later Presidents.

THE WASHINGTON PAPER

EXTRA

FRIDAY, MARCH 29, 1907

5 CENTS

ISSUE 47

STOCK MARKET CRASHES

47

Also, trust company directors were often involved in banks, and the

Biff: By the time he left office, Theodore Roosevelt was the world's most popular man. After he helped an old friend William Taft get elected, he went on a year long African safari.

Ruby: Then he and his wife, Edith, made a three month tour in Europe.

Pete: When he finished his European trip and returned home, Mr. Roosevelt was unhappy that President Taft had slowed down many of his reforms.

Biff: Yes. In fact, he was so unhappy that he decided to challenge President Taft for the party's 1912 nomination. This hurt their friendship and split the Republican Party.

Pete: But Mr. Roosevelt won the primaries and even defeated President Taft in Taft's home state of Ohio.

Biff: Is anyone surprised that Theodore Roosevelt would then help form a new political party called The Progressive Party? It was nicknamed the 'Bull Moose Party.'

Pete: This was the first major political party that wanted to give women the right to vote.

Ruby: I forgot that women didn't have the right to vote, yet.

Can't Stop This Bull Moose

Pete: Look out! There's a man with a gun in the crowd.

Biff: On October 14th, 1912, Teddy Roosevelt was shot on his way to a speech. The bullet went through his overcoat and clothes and was slowed as it hit a folded, forty-two page speech, and tin case that held his glasses.

Pete: Lucky for him.

Ruby: This is amazing. He's giving a speech despite being wounded and bleeding.

Theodore Roosevelt: It takes more than a bullet to stop a Bull Moose.

Biff: When the Democratic candidate, Woodrow Wilson won, Mr. Roosevelt decided to form an expedition and explore the Amazon River.

Pete: It seems he always eased his defeats by traveling. But wasn't he getting too old for such an adventure?

Theodore Roosevelt: I had to go. It was my last chance to be a boy!

Ruby: He injured his leg on the dangerous rapids and was infected with malaria.

Pete: Wasn't that a dangerous, life threatening disease?

Biff: Yes. The poor man lost fifty pounds in eight weeks which aged him drastically, but he made it back alive.

Biff: After an amazing life, Theodore Roosevelt died peacefully in his sleep on January 6th, 1919.

Pete: Theodore Roosevelt was a great President during an exciting time in our history.

Ruby: It'll be easy to write my report on this fascinating President.

Biff: Then, let's head back home. We're Buffalo Biff and Farley's Raiders.

All: Yahoo!

There's much more to learn about Theodore Roosevelt
on the internet or at your local library.

Now it's your chance to become the character
of your choice in this Time Traveler's Adventure.
Get ready and have fun becoming one of

Farley's Raiders!